LETS
GO
PUBLISH!

Sources

http://www.americanchronicle.com/articles/534-- Illegal Aliens and Immigration, June 3, 2005

http://www.americanchronicle.com/articles/613-- All Immigration problems Solved, June 11, 2005

http://www.americanchronicle.com/articles/2884-- Labor Arbitrage? Better Known as Cheap Labor, October 12, 2005

http://www.americanchronicle.com/articles/3693 -- Coin of the Realm, November 14, 2005

Great Political Essays
from
Thomas Dawson

Thomas Dawson writes from the heart and the soul

Ten years ago, when I wrote a book titled *Taxation without Representation*, in my research, I discovered four great essays by Thomas Dawson that fit the purposes of my book. I included all four essays as separate chapters in the book. Mr. Thomas Dawson was very kind in granting me permission to use his well-written essays in the book and I expressed my appreciation.

In the 4th Edition of the book, I could no longer find Dawson's essays at the chronicle.com website which is now defunct. So, I decided that I would release his essays under a separate title rather than bury them in the middle of my book. I wrote Mr. Dawson again and the email did not bounce back but I received no acknowledgment for this recent request.

They address areas in which all of us have an interest—immigration, illegal foreign nationals, cheap labor, unions, and greedy corporations. I hope you enjoy these essays as much as I.

Edited and annotated by

B R I A N   W.   K E L L Y

LETS
GO
PUBLISH

Disclaimer: Though judicious care was taken throughout the writing and the publication of this work that the information contained herein is accurate, there is no expressed or implied warranty that all information in this book is 100% correct. Therefore, neither LETS GO PUBLISH, nor the author accepts liability for any use of this work.

Trademarks: A number of products and names referenced in this book are trade names and trademarks of their respective companies. For example, iSeries and AS/400 are trademarks of the IBM Corporation and Windows is a trademark of Microsoft Corporation.

Referenced Material : The information in this book has been obtained through personal and third party observations and copious reading over many years. Where unique information has been provided or extracted from other sources, those sources are acknowledged within the text of the book itself. Thus, there are no formal footnotes nor is there a bibliography section.

Published by: LETS GO PUBLISH!
               Brian P. Kelly, Publisher
               P.O. Box 161
               Wilkes-Barre, PA 18703
               brian@brianpkelly.com
               www.letsgopublish.com

Library of Congress Copyright Information Pending

Book Cover Design by Brian W. Kelly

ISBN Information: The International Standard Book Number (ISBN) is a unique machine-readable identification number, which marks any book unmistakably. The ISBN is the clear standard in the book industry. 159 countries and territories are officially ISBN members. The Official ISBN for this book is:

978-1-947402-28-7

The price for this work is: $6.95 USD

10   9   8   7   6   5   4   3   2   1

Release Date: January 2018

Dedication

*To Brian Patrick, Michael Patrick,
Kathleen Patricia*

My Wonderful Children

*At the Top of All My Lists for a Long
Time!*

And Forever!

Acknowledgments

I appreciate all the help that I have received in putting this book together as well as all of my 145 other published books, which I have written and / or edited. .

My printed acknowledgments had become so large that book readers "complained" about going through too many pages to get to page one of the text.

And, so to permit me more flexibility, I put my acknowledgment list online, and it continues to grow. Believe it or not, it once cost about a dollar more to print each book.

Thank you and God bless you all for your help.

Please check out www.letsgopublish.com to read the latest version of my heartfelt acknowledgments updated for this book. FYI, Wily Ky Eyely loves this book and recommends it to all other 11-year old little Maesters

Click the bottom of the Main menu!

Thank you all!\

Table of Contents

Preface:

Nothing stands still in time including the effects of illegal immigration with 60 million illegal residents today in the US. President Trump has a big job in cleaning up the mess left by the Bush Administration and the Obama Administration. We wish him well.

Thomas Dawson took the time in 2005 to write four poignant essays about the dilemmas that the US faced after the half-way mark of the Bush Presidency. Though this was well past 9/11/2001, America was a more cautious country. The threat of Terrorism and the Iraq and Afghanistan Wars were not the only things facing the US. There were also big problems on the domestic side. These include legal and illegal immigration, 60 million illegal foreign nationals in residence, cheap labor, unions, and greedy corporations.

Unlike many of us, Thomas Dawson faithfully examined these issues and he did a masterful job in explaining them to all Americans when his essays were published in the American Chronicle in 2005.

I think you will enjoy this book and I hope that it inspires you to think through America's major issues and to help our Congress work to solve these problems for the good of all Americans.

I wish you the best,

Brian W. Kelly, Editor

About the Editor

Brian W. Kelly retired as an Assistant Professor in the Business Information Technology (BIT) program at Marywood University, where he also served as the IBM i; and Midrange Systems technical advisor to the IT faculty. Kelly has designed, developed, and taught many college and professional courses. He is also a contributing technical editor to a number of IT industry magazines, including "The Four Hundred" and "Four Hundred Guru" published by IT Jungle.

Kelly is a former IBM Senior Systems Engineer and he still has an active information technology consultancy. He is the author of 145 books and numerous articles. Kelly has been a frequent speaker at COMMON, IBM conferences, and other technical conferences.

In 2010, Kelly ran for Congress as a Democrat against a 13-term Democrat and, took no campaign contributions, spent enough to buy signs and T-shirts, and as a virtual unknown, he captured 17% of the vote.

Chapter 1 Essays from Thomas Dawson: Introduction

Taxation and Representation

There may be some topics that you find in this book that do not seem to go with the theme of taxation and representation such as immigration. Wouldn't it be nice if our tax money was not used to lure foreigners to our shores and then pay their way? Would it not be nice if we had representation about whether we should support people from other countries before our representatives took what they wanted from our wallets? So, yes, immigration has lots to do with taxation and representation—or the lack thereof.

Would it not be nice if corporations played fairly with wages and with their hiring practices? What's wrong with America-first?

Surprise in Email

While I was researching the first edition of a book titled Taxation Without Representation, now in its 4th edition, I came across numerous anecdotes, many of which were nothing short of amazing and phenomenally insightful. One thing I have learned in my 69 years (my 70th Birthday is on its way) is that nobody knows it all and as a corollary, there is something brilliant that is always out there, ready to be discovered every day.

I was so impressed with the writings of Thomas Dawson, both in content and style that I wrote him a few months before the first edition was completed, and asked if I could use his material in this book. At the time, I had intended to use some excerpts of his works in the main body of some of the chapters in which his insights applied. But, when I received Tom's note right before I submitted the first edition, I had to make other arrangements.

I thought about an insertion here or there and then I decided that, since Mr. Dawson offered no strings on his granting permission for the use of his works, I would print them as his essays for your reading pleasure and give him the full credit he deserves.

His work is so well received that I decided to create a books just to display his fine essays.

This was his note to me. I have never met him, but you can feel the goodness of this gentleman in his words:

Mr. Kelly:

Sorry I couldn't get back to you sooner. You are more than welcome to use any of my material at your discretion, either in agreement with my thinking or in disagreement. You need not give credit. This old bumpkin will be delighted if you can encourage someone to think about the world in which the next generation will live. Provoke thought whenever possible.

I wish you personal satisfaction in your endeavors, and please inform me when your book is available.

With warm regards

Tom

How can you beat that? So I took the poetic license to provide four of Thomas Dawson's essays from 2005 from the American Chronicle. Unfortunately, they are no longer available as the site is no longer operational. Please enjoy and encourage others to think about the world in which the next generation will live. Provoke thought whenever possible.

Difficulties lie ahead

These works of Thomas Dawson are really well done. I wish I can meet Mr. Dawson one day. He is a real patriot. They are good pieces for you to have in your personal library and there is good news. There are a number of other works by Thomas Dawson on the Internet available for your reading. When I find where the treasure trove of Mr. Dawson's writing is hosted, I will update this book in paperback and in Kindle form so that you can access them directly.

They all tell a story like my book, about taxation without representation. Mr. Dawson granted his approval to offer a similar thought as his on the subject and he offered me the opportunity to take issue with him. Very gracious!

Obviously, I wrote my book to point out the travesty and the reality of taxation without representation in the modern age. Topics from taxes to the fact that hizzoners, all over the U.S. at all levels of government, who are not representing the American people, make up the bulk of the book.

The culprit in most cases is the corporation in cohort with the government but with major complicity of our "honorables." If I were Thomas Dawson, I would have said that the purpose of this book is to "encourage someone to think about the world in which the next generation will live. Provoke thought whenever possible." Of course, that is exactly what he told me to do.

I predict these essays will be a treat for you to read. I love reading them. Dawson hits all issues hard but never below the belt. The issues in the essays just as the issues raised in my book are not yet solved but each person who reads Dawson's fine essays will be extra motivated to help.

There are big problems to solve. Mr. Dawson points these issues out in his essays. We have a lot of work to do in helping our brothers and sisters in America take back control of our government. It won't be easy. But, with the risk of having Nancy Pelosi, Chuck Schumer in charge of our lives for what would seem like an eternity, we must take action now.

I will sign off my part of this book right now, leaving you in the hands of Mr. Thomas Dawson for the next four chapters. Know that the difficulties ahead are solvable if we watchfully pay attention to our government and call it to task on what it must do. I feel confident leaving you to these essays and then to yourself and all the other selves like you and I, and Thomas Dawson, an American Patriot.

God Bless You -- and our America.

Chapter 2 Illegal Aliens and Immigration

By Thomas Dawson

June 03, 2005

Americans want the problem solved

We do not have an immigration problem with Mexico. We do have a border problem with Mexico. Without making more jokes about Homeland Security, borders are important. Without borders, there is no country…or security. Some public political debate has begun, but don't expect too much. The easiest way to win a political argument in today's world, particularly if your position is without practical merit is to confuse the issues.

The proponents of open borders, and there are many, use this method to make their arguments. They never use the correct term "illegal alien". They refuse to view these people as either illegal or aliens. The most that one can hope for, is that they will use the term "undocumented immigrants". You can bet that after one or two minutes of discussion the term will degenerate into just "immigrants". Without any qualifier, most of what they say is correct. Most importantly, whatever you say in their context sounds racist. Of course, we live in an age of labels and buzzwords. If you allow such people to get away with it, they will play the game of "gotcha" as they try to stick a label on you. Unfortunately, this is not a child's game.

If the media polls are correct, the American people overwhelmingly recognize the gravity of the situation and would like to correct it. We're not talking about Democrats or Republicans here nor Conservatives or Liberals. When we take the labels off, you'll find that most American citizens can and often do, think!

Alas, there is little hope for any real change to take place in the near future. There is a great and growing disconnect between modern politicians and the people they are supposedly representing. So there will be a great deal of gamesmanship or slight of hand to convince people that they are looking into the situation. In reality, the politicians will continue to stall any useful action for the sake of their "financial constituency".

Some discussion at the federal level has finally begun again, and a few really big political names are making a lot of noise. But in a typical stalling tactic, the discussion is not about closing the borders. The talk is about those illegal aliens that are already here and many more that will come, as we make plans for them.

Their only concern is what will be the final criteria to make them underclass citizens? Discussions with this kind of detailed minutia can be dragged out for a very long time… and they will be. Meanwhile, Vicente Fox is sending us as many of his people as he can; as fast as he can.

The federal politicians are beholden to organized interest groups for financial support and really find it difficult, if not impossible to stand up for their people 'back home' on any major issue where a lot of corporate money is at stake.

Amnesty for Mexican illegal aliens was granted a few years ago, and since then the border control has been relaxed. Now we are being told that there is no alternative for a humane solution without again providing amnesty. Don't listen to the politicians; they have no intention of closing the Mexican borders until, and only if forced to do so. It is only a ploy to bring in more cheap labor for exploitation.

The failed corporate religion of Globalization in the name of 'free trade' is really a search for the cheapest labor available. Corporations have greased the wheels of government and momentum is steamrolling any public opposition.

Manufacturers are now allowed to 'globalize' by outsourcing their labor costs to the cheapest of overseas labor, and retailers can 'globalize' by purchasing the cheapest products they can find manufactured overseas, and thus they can both increase their profits.

They can also claim increases in productivity in a single stroke as they reduce their costs. The question arises. Why should agriculture and service industries that cannot move overseas not share in Globalization? The simple answer is they can. Simply have the politicians "move the mountain to Mohammed".

Now that the government allows corporations to bring in really cheap "illegals" for the service and agriculture industries, they too are receiving the labor/cost benefits of 'Globalization'. Not to mention the hundreds of thousands of "guest workers" that have already been imported to work as engineers, IT technicians, etc which are hired at only 50% to

80% of the going rate in this country, thus holding down the wage scales of the middle class and increasing corporate profits. With a single stroke of the pen and government grease, anything can be made legal. Seems like a sensible way to reduce wages and push profits up.

To paraphrase Milton Friedman, "Corporate executives, provided they stay within the law, have no responsibilities in their business activities other than to make as much money for their stockholders as possible." Milton Freeman is absolutely right.

A corporation has no responsibility to anyone. It is not a person. It is a legal animal (entity) created by the law of a country. It is an animal without social conscience or concern for anything except profits. If a corporation has any responsibility, it is only to the law of the country in which it operates. It is the duty of the country of origin to regulate and control its offspring.

When a domestic corporation behaves badly, it should be disciplined. When a foreign company behaves badly, it should be disciplined and if it continues, refrained from doing business. Every country should set the rules for its own house.

If we allow "globalization" to wring out our middle class, we can easily lose the increased standard of living gained during the first quarter century after World War II. (Since then. our standard of living has gone nowhere. It has probably even declined a bit in the last quarter century.)

Our problem is not with the natural ambitions of corporations. Our problem is with the deliberately calibrated reluctance of (the peoples?) representation in government to regulate with any care for or concern toward the public good.

In the long run though, the politicians at the state and local levels will have to face the reality of the economic situation. Continuing to assume low cost, near poverty level labor has a depressing effect on all wages over extended periods of time. Increases in poverty create demand for state and local services as well as lowering per capita taxes. Hospitals across the south to California have had to go into bankruptcy and some have closed because of expenses incurred by illegal aliens who are unable to pay.

Many immigrants and illegal aliens have earnings low enough to qualify for welfare assistance. At the same time, these states and local governments are experiencing lower per capita tax revenues as wages begin to drift downwards.

The greatest increase in costs due to these illegal aliens and low cost immigrants is, of course education. Law enforcement and incarceration costs are also rising.

It is estimated that in 2003, California alone, even after accounting for tax contributions from illegal aliens, the direct cost was more than $8,000,000,000 and total costs probably well in excess of $11,000,000,000. California can't even fix their roads, and this is just the beginning! All this is just part of the cost of subsidizing labor for the service industries.

As we erode the middle class and the consumer market begins to falter, the tax base will continue to shrink and tax revenues fall. After all, middle class working people pay the vast bulk of the tax burden. What will your town look like as state and local governments slash services by 15, 20, or even 25%?

Increasing numbers of illegal aliens and poverty level immigrants cause economic and social disruption. On the other hand, carefully managed legal immigration will contribute to the economic and social growth of the country. Bringing in large numbers of qualified people to fill jobs (at current rates of pay) where there are labor or professional shortages means more contributing citizens. Encouraging carefully managed increases in immigration is important to this country, both as an economic contribution and by increasing the population underpinning.

Do we have problems in agriculture? Certainly! How many people do we need to help us out? The government says that we already have between eight and a half million and eleven million illegal aliens. Others estimate between eighteen and twenty million. [Brian Kelly estimates 60 million.] The likely probability is that we have between twelve and fifteen million.

This means that the illegal aliens represent about four percent or slightly more of our population. This is about one out of every twenty-five people. Should we bring in more people for every crop and then let them melt into the general population and continue to grow a permanent underclass of cheap labor, undermining the wage base of the entire country? Of course not!

There must be a constant, but controlled rotation of workers for agriculture. Perhaps permanent labor arrangements could be had with foreign labor at a slightly better rate of pay. Assuming we want to continue to subsidize agriculture with cheap labor, there are a number of possibilities.

Alternatively, we may want to consider taking the gratuitous profits away from corporate owners of our subsidized, socialized agricultural enterprises. Or perhaps even doing away with socialized agriculture and even corporate welfare entirely! I am sure that politicians would find this to be a national security issue far greater than merely open borders! But that is a subject for another day.

Even if we continue to subsidize agriculture with (dare I say dirt cheap) labor, this does not mean that every business should be entitled to hire at poverty wage levels. Inviting immigration at or near poverty level wages is not good for this country's public good. Let the service businesses pay a little more and charge a little more. We can pay more for the services or pay a lot more for the subsidies.

Workers in the construction trades have been a part of the middle class for the last fifty years. Now, with the strongest continuous housing boom and the highest prices for houses in our history, construction workers are experiencing falling wages and unemployment due to unemployed cheap and often illegal labor. It's past time to consider where we are heading.

It's also time to close our borders and then begin a serious discussion. In any case, any political talk about solving the immigration problem without first closing the borders is pure deception, and a sham!

Chapter 3 All Immigration Problems Solved

By Thomas Dawson

June 11, 2005

Is globalization the problem or the answer

A panel set up by the Counsel on Foreign Relations wants Americans to stop thinking of themselves as United States citizens and to think of themselves as just North Americans. The panel has published a report called "Building a North American Community" in which it proposes a single common border around the three countries.

The purpose is to create a free flow of goods and labor between the countries. They hope to accomplish this over the next five years, by 2010.

It seems unfortunate that Asia is not adjacent to us so that they could provide even larger numbers of even cheaper labor for the corporate citizens of this new world order, that has now completely bought out our government.

In reality, this is just another salvo in the battle to create an aura of inevitability around the idea of globalization. The destruction of borders for the purpose of moving cheap labor is only one facet of this new deity. If we can be convinced that we are caught up in the inevitable tide of history, then the right to choose has been taken from us.

It has become the obligation of our highly paid government officials to prepare the middle class citizens for changes that their employers intend to make in this world. Certainly, if they can pull it off, this would be a great step forward toward globalization. In any case, these kinds of discussions create another great stall to keep the borders open.

Globalization, the idea of a 'One World Government" is not new. We fought WWII so that the world would not become fascist. We endured the cold war so that the world would not become communist. Since then we have worried that the UN would take over the world and form a world government. Now we find that the seeds of our cultural destruction are to be found in the very basis of our democratic free enterprise system.

This country has always indulged the corporate community as one of our children, giving it status, favoring it over any other public interest. We have asked little in return.

We mistakenly assumed that in return for this favored status, these entities would naturally provide employment for our citizens with wages sufficient to sustain an improving standard of living in the long run. For the past thirty years we have considered failure in this regard as only a temporary setback. Now we find that sustaining a reasonable standard of living or even the continued employment of middle class citizens is not on the agenda, not even a consideration of the corporate community.

Unfortunately, this unwritten contract or understanding does not exist in principle any more than it does in writing. What did we expect? We have failed to discipline this child of ours and now it has become a self-serving tyrant. You probably thought the "Robber Barons" were tough. I can assure you that, as Ronald Reagan would say "You ain't seen nothing yet!"

We are spectators to the birthing of this new world order called Globalization. Large international corporations, which even now are no longer responsible to, nor contributing to any public good, have high hopes of running the world as a single cooperative trading entity.

The very concept of traditional nation-states will become irrelevant. Large trading companies will run this brave new world on an "as needed" basis. Nation-states will become reduced to mere cultural centers. These will become the transport systems of the trading companies, with which they will trade in people and goods wherever required. A managers' dream! Indeed, the managers are already, at this very moment, the aristocrats of our time. Globalization is to become the manifestation of their consolidation of power.

Managers have already replaced the capitalists and entrepreneurs in the world of international corporations. Only minor players and small companies are still willing or need to risk their money in today's environment. International companies do not invest in new enterprises or attempt to compete with other companies.

They either buy out small companies that appear to be successful within a given market, or merge with their competitors. In either case, market share is increased and a secure established market is acquired without risk. Little is left to chance; they are managing everything; most especially the governments of the western world. Management has finally trumped leadership in business, as well as in government.

To be sure, at the moment they still need other companies with whom they can appear to compete. This is not an overt conspiracy. It is rather, a "gentleman's agreement"; an understanding, if you will. For the moment, at least, the illusion of competition must be maintained. But, consider that just this week, Toyota is taking the poison pill because they fear someone will take them over due to their recent financial success.

In the dawn of this global environment, the realization of any entrepreneurial success will probably become sufficient reason for your immediate demise, as expanding international interests will try to gobble you up. Our enormous financial institutions will even provide money for little fish to eat big fish, providing the big fish have control over secure markets. Because of the low risk factor in these kinds of takeovers, these financial institutions only require a relative premium over the current interest rate.

The United States has been an easy mark for the globalization movement due to the close ties developed by corporations between themselves and financially dependent and greedy government officials, readily managed by corporate money. These corporations are, to our elected representatives, their "financial constituents". The pharmaceutical industry alone has two people lobbying on every congressman.

Asian countries may not be so easy; they only needed corporate connections with the west until they were locked into the relatively affluent western economies. They have the world's largest cheap labor force and are now graduating great numbers of highly educated people. They will soon have the largest and cheapest well-educated work force in the world.

Their economies have gained momentum and as they grow, they become somewhat insulated and independent of western style corporate persuasion. They will appear to tolerate a certain amount of corporate "rule making" such as "intellectual property" only so long as it serves their interests. They understand the greed of our corporations and are happily building "feed lots" for them. When all is said and done, Asia will not view these international corporations as their own children, to be coddled and upon whom they will stake their future.

When these corporations have been fattened and can no longer contribute to the national interest, their assets will be nationalized; gobbled up by some "really big fish" that are hardly manageable.

Chapter 4 Labor Arbitrage? Better Known as Cheap Labor

By Thomas Dawson

October 12, 2005

How low can wages go?

It's time we stopped kidding ourselves! The continuation of the illegal immigration from Mexico is the direct intention of our government. When a government enforces a law, we are inclined to think that the enforcement is their duty.

However, when a government does not enforce the law, we are inclined to think that perhaps it is their choice. It is not. Not when it concerns the security of our borders. Of course there are reasons for our government's overt support for the illegal immigration on the southern border.

Since the end of the 'Cold War', our international companies have turned their attention and swayed the attention of our government toward the domination of world economics without concern for the domestic consequences. This variation on the economic system is referred to as the neo-liberal economic system and is generally understood as globalization.

It is part and parcel of the modern democratic theory as expounded by the United States and is to be imposed upon the rest of the world, by force if necessary. Even our children understand by now that globalization favors corporate profits above the common good, or anything else.

The most obvious example of the effects of globalization in this country is our relationship with Asia. Over the past few years, we have not only outsourced our jobs, but have moved our manufacturing to the Asian countries, especially China and India. Corporate money has influenced our government to allow the transfer of practically any business into these new rising economies at the expense of American jobs. There are two major reasons for this interest. First, Asia is seen as the future of economic progress because of their tremendous population and potential buying power. Second, labor and manufacturing plant is so cheap that exorbitant profits can be made when Asian manufactures are sold here; at American prices of course.

It is not difficult to understand that when the cost of plant and equipment is about half of the costs required in the United States, and labor costs are only 10% of the costs in the United States, corporations will naturally choose to manufacture in Asia. Our government officials are no longer concerned about the common good of its citizens; rather they are interested in their personal gain to be acquired through corporate influence.

At home, our service industries can only exist as long as there is enough money circulating among the middle and lower classes to support the consumerism. Our financial industry can only continue to exist as long as the asset bubble continues.

Our only real source of income is our military weapons business. We supply most of the world's weapons. Where does the money come from to maintain our economy? It is the consistent growth of our national and personal debts that maintains the momentum of our economy. Our government needs to maintain that momentum for a while longer.

As far as our corporations are concerned, the writing is on the wall. Real, or long-term investment will be made in Asia where a huge population with rising incomes will eventually dominate the economic world. The unemployed population in China alone is greater than the entire population of the United States.

As the income of the average American citizen continues to erode, we are viewed by the corporate world as a mature market. The United States is no longer a prime market for investment. It is time to reap the profits of past investments and maintain the cash cow as long as possible, or at least until a prosperous Asian economy can be built. Unfortunately, it is obvious that our government supports this corporate view, regardless of what their lips tell us.

A few years ago, these investments would not have happened. There were laws against unfair trade, concerning environmental issues, unfair labor practices, and a plethora of other rules and considerations for the public good. In the past few years many of these laws have been expunged or relaxed in the name of deregulation to allow for the international exploitation of labor. This is our government at work in behalf of their corporate constituencies.

Lest they lose their corporate sponsors, our media is now blaming Asia and especially China for the loss of our jobs and their excessive use of 'our' oil. It is our own government that encourages companies to invest in foreign countries, even to the point of awarding tax breaks for doing so.

It is our own government that is encouraging the displacement of American workers with cheaper foreign workers. China is not the villain here. It is our own government encouraging and aiding international corporations to move their business overseas in search of that Holy Grail, profits.

What about corporations that are not international in nature? Our government is doing its best to take care of them as well. It has deliberately brought in well over twenty million illegal Mexicans to work at menial wages and continues to dilute the work force. Of course, the government will explain that farm labor is still in short supply and we need more workers there. It seems that 'illegals' don't want to farm either.

They are coming in faster than the great immigration of the late nineteenth and early twentieth century. To be sure many of them eventually earn more than minimum wages.

However, they can secure few, if any rights and are treated poorly. They do not generally get health benefits, nor do they get retirement benefits. Just as the international companies can exploit cheap labor, a similar arrangement has been made for the national companies. Labor is arbitraged just as any other commodity.

Our population is estimated at somewhat less than three hundred million people. If we have only twenty million illegal immigrants, it means that one out of every fifteen people in this country is illegal. It is a significantly higher portion in the work force.

Notice that even in the rebuilding of New Orleans, the prevailing labor rates will not be paid to workers. The contracts will be generally given out without competitive bidding at cost plus, to insure corporate profits to preferred companies. Restricting labor expenses will be the only means to hold down costs. For some strange reason there seems to be a shortage of workers. The government is bringing people willing to work from Central America. Is this because construction is just one more type of work that Americans won't do? Many of them will probably remain in this country to further dilute the work force. Meanwhile the poor of New Orleans have been dispersed around the country and will probably not be heard from again.

Reducing labor costs is the mantra of our time. This first attempt to dismantle Social Security is only the beginning. Many of our corporations are hiring illegal immigrants and do not pay any benefits. Other corporations will soon be crying that they cannot compete if they have to pay for health benefits or pension plans or perhaps even paid holidays.

Our government intends to get cheap labor for their corporations by leveling the labor of the world at the expense of the American citizen. We have embraced a Darwinian system of economics to the detriment of our citizens! Or is this the Intelligent Design at work? In either case, it looks like plain old government sponsored greed.

Chapter 5 The Coin of the Realm

By Thomas Dawson

November 14, 2005

Corporations have no hearts, no flesh, and no soul

Since World War II our political entanglements with the rest of the world have been increasingly, rightly or wrongly, intended to secure or engender the business interests of our corporations. Suddenly our international companies are enamored with the opportunities to move labor-intensive segments of their business to foreign lands. They now view the United States as only a temporary cash cow; a mature market to be used until faster growing markets can be developed elsewhere.

At the same time, the interests of these corporations, who indirectly control our domestic economy, are often at odds with the welfare of our middle class. Corporate America has bought and paid for the influence of our politicians and since the end of the "cold war" they have been systematically reducing their liabilities and responsibilities with respect to the people that work for them in the quest for greater profits.

The primary and driving force of corporations is profit and this is as it should be. These corporations make up the engine of the American economy. However, the continued displacement of middle class jobs, which are flowing out of the country at alarming rates, and the eroding standard of living, are the result of this same kind of thinking, and is encouraged by our present political structure. But, lest we forget, these United States were not intended as a land "of the corporation, by the corporation and for the corporation".

The national debt, trade deficits, middle class wage erosion, immigration problems, health care costs, and a plethora of other national problems are all related to the political reality of "American style free trade" expanding throughout the world in the last quarter century.

We are told that these are normal, sequential economic changes taking place within our political system. Not so. The primary causation of most of these changes is the direct result of political pandering to corporate interests by our elected officials. Legislation should have some consideration of the "people" mentioned by our founding fathers.

The standard of living for the middle class in this country has not improved in the last quarter century. In fact, it has declined for the vast majority of Americans. Real wages have fallen more than 6%. Yet the GNP really is up! Because our (domestic?) companies are really making record profits! Our corporations are awash in money. At the same time the country is currently acquiring nearly THREE BILLION dollars of new debt through the trade deficit every day!

Consider the National Debt. Disgraceful, and dangerous! A lot of other things are also going on here. This is a direct result of political pandering for corporate money. Politics is a very lucrative "profession". (Hardly anyone is doing this as a public service)

The truth is that politicians cannot survive without hoards of money. Ask anyone who has ever run for office how much it costs. Certainly the man on the street cannot support them. So where do they get it? Who has it? Only large corporations can make large contributions regularly over long periods of time. Most of it is given to the party's themselves so they can keep members in line through the use of the money spigot.

Not so long ago, this seemed like a reasonably good idea. Most of the large companies were entirely domestic and employed many people. The import/export companies were either bringing money into the country or buying products not available here. Many companies took on an international flavor while we were rebuilding Europe and Japan after WWII with their captive markets.

Large amounts of money were acquired by American companies, along with a great deal of knowledge about other countries' economies and politics. Great sums of money were spent on R&D and any new technology from around the world was developed quickly by the large US companies.

All this employment was one of the major factors in building the American middle class. "What's good for General Motors is good for the Country" seemed to be a pretty accurate phrase if not an accurate quote. A direct connection between domestic GNP and the domestic standard of living was just assumed to be the natural condition. Unfortunately, in a few short years, this assumption would be ruptured.

In the middle 50's and 60's we began to see some interesting changes. We began to increase the imports of foreign goods, and some of our companies began to build plants in foreign countries and even exported products back home. Volkswagen began to sell cars over here. We could now buy an English Ford. This was good business for everyone. Business around the world was heating up. Everyone seemed to understand the rules and we all did well.

The Japanese suddenly burst on the scene. By the end of the 70's and into the 80's their quality cars were the best buy for the money. They had the best quality and Americans bought them. American car companies had manipulated the auto market for years for their own benefit and now the Japanese were encroaching on their very survival.

Fortunately, Reagan was made to understand that we could not just watch such a large section of the middle class workforce go down the drain. He effectively limited the number of Japanese imports. When the Japanese asked to build automobiles over here and employ Americans, he invited them in.

It was not the corporation he was protecting, it was the middle class American workforce. (This ridiculous, Pro-American concern for the citizen did not go unnoticed by our growing international corporations and was soon to be changed.) The American manufacturers quickly improved the quality of their products and regained much of their reputation. Again, business was good for everybody.

Many corporations, especially those with international interests became extremely powerful as they did more business than many countries. It is only natural that they would want to extend their influence. For corporations this large, there is only one place of effective influence and that is the politician, domestic and foreign.

As large corporations are always looking for a profit advantage, they could hardly help noticing the disparity in wages between the developed countries and the under-developed ones. Japan has no natural resources and cannot compete with countries that do. They have to import, add value, and then export to make a profit. Business was so good that as their standard of living rose and they were over-employed, they "outsourced" the labor and for a few years had an enviable economy (read corporate profits). (Remember Japan bashing?) Other international companies soon began to follow when the "cold war" came to a close.

This kind of business was obviously not within the range of Reagan's pro-American thinking, but who cared? Corporations were making plenty of money and political contributions were rolling in! By the end of the 90's the world economy had so heated up that politicians easily convinced us that outsourcing cheap labor would not hurt the developed countries and that it would be of great benefit to the under-developed ones if only work rules, environmental considerations, and other regulations would be removed. (How benevolent they had become!)

Besides, their corporate benefactors could make a lot of money. We were having a domestic technology boom not unlike the automotive boom of the twenties. The slow-down (recession) of the early 90's seemed like a blip in an ever-growing world economic boom.

To really make the corporations happy, the government got into the act with a bill to open so-called "free trade zones". And thus, NAFTA was born. This bill was sold as raising the Mexican standard of living and creating thousands of American jobs. A win, win bill!

No one seriously believed American jobs would be created! In just a few short years this labor arbitrage has reduced the average wage in Mexico to about half of what it was before NAFTA. Our corporations were doing very well, because now they had something just as good as or perhaps better than a free trade zone.

They arranged another form of arbitrage, outsourcing their labor to Asian countries. Why pay 50 cents an hour to a Mexican when the Asians will work for 25 cents? The politicians even found ways to pay their corporate benefactors to outsource, by offering them tax breaks for doing it! No one can compete with Corporate America! Certainly the American citizen can't!

Big farm Corporations have been trying to control congress since the 1930's. They have learned well and now other large corporations emulate them. All kinds of moneys are spent by the farm lobbies on strong incumbent congressmen and their families to "educate them" on the reasons for, and the importance of farm subsidies and other corporate interests.

Along with his family and personal 'educational' benefits, the incumbent congressman will often get considerable moneys as contributions to his election campaign. Even larger contributions are made to his party (both parties for control purposes); of which his share will trickle down to him from a number of sources as long as he does not depart from the party interests (read corporate interests).

It's not hard to get a Congressman from Iowa to support a farm subsidy bill. It's a little harder to get a Delaware or Massachusetts Congressman to support it. One might think that this would take a bit of doing, as many times the congressman must support those things that are a direct detriment to his voting constituents.

Most of the time however, his opponent will not even challenge him on these highly financed issues because his own funds from the party are controlled at a higher level. This system works so well that even pharmaceutical companies now spend rafts of money to "educate" doctors and their families at various resorts around the country. Currently, the pharmaceuticals are even "donating" to the FDA (for our benefit, of course). Understand that politicians can and do pass laws to benefit themselves, this is all perfectly legal

At this point in time, the voter has been effectively disenfranchised. It is not that he does not have a choice; it is only that there is no choice. Whoever runs for office is beholden to the corporations for the money that is a necessary prerequisite to attain and retain the office. This, in effect, is the new democratic "one party" or "corporate party" system.

The politician and his family live in a world filled with both perks and promise. If he cooperates and is in office for any considerable length of time, he is practically guaranteed a plum lifetime job consulting or lobbying for these same companies and thus greasing the wheels of other politicians. (Responsible companies always reward their good soldiers.)

The heavy hand of corporate influence on the members of congress is not a new problem. It has been a festering problem since the earliest days of our country. When the great majority of citizens were farmers, it didn't seem that lobbyists could do much harm. As corporate America grew and farming became more efficient, the trend was for more Americans to leave the farms and become employees of these new corporations.

In the last part of the nineteenth century, thinking people were becoming concerned that the interests of Corporate America and the country as a whole were not of a like nature. There was much concern that corporate money was controlling the outcome of most of the laws in this country, and something should be done to curb this influence.

In his annual message to the congress in 1907, President Theodore Roosevelt stated "The need for collecting large campaign funds would vanish if Congress provided an appropriation for the proper and legitimate expenses of each of the great national parties, an appropriation ample enough to meet the necessity for thorough organization and machinery, which requires a great expenditure of money.

Then the stipulation should be made that no party receiving campaign funds from the Treasury should accept more than a fixed amount from any individual subscriber or donor, and the necessary publicity for receipts and expenditures could without difficulty be provided." This is an idea that is still mentioned from time to time.

Many, if not most of the legislation that is enacted helps one group of people at the expense of another. Such is the nature of laws. Laws against cartels and monopolies in favor of fairness to the other corporations and indeed the citizens are necessary and good for the health of our country, but only if the government chooses to enforce them.

Laws passed against the middle class Americans in favor of powerful corporations are not good for the health of our country. In theory, the elected officials are supposed to represent the voting public, not the corporate contributors. Passing legislation that will erode the middle class for the benefit of corporate profits is a crime against the citizenry.

You cannot blame a rat as a thief if you allow it to steal grain, nor blame a cat as a murderer if you allow it to kill rats. That is the very nature of these animals. You cannot blame corporations if you allow them to buy politicians. This is indeed the very nature of this animal. To paraphrase Milton Friedman, "Corporate executives, provided they stay within the law, have no responsibilities in their business activities other than to make as much money for their stockholders as possible."

That is why we need laws and regulations, to determine exactly what is to be allowed. You can and should blame politicians for selling out their trust of the people. No longer does anyone except perhaps some relatives and political associates hold politicians in high regard. That is why we need laws and regulations, to determine exactly what is to be allowed and what is not.

You can and should blame corrupt politicians for selling out their trust of the people. They are committing overt crimes against the voters of these United States. Politics and Crime have become two faces of the same coin. Unfortunately, in the United States it has become coin of the realm.

Other books by Brian Kelly: (amazon.com, and Kindle)

Taxation Without Representation Can the US Afford Another Tea Party?
Delete the EPA You won't believe what they are up to now!
Wipe Out All Student Debt Now! How to improve the economy with one bold move
 Boost Social Security Now! Hey Buddy Can You Spare a Dime?
The Birth of American Football. From the first college game in 1869 to the last Super Bowl
Obamacare: A One-Line Repeal Congress must get this done.
A Wilkes-Barre Christmas Story A wonderful town makes Christmas all the better
A Boy, A Bike, A Train, and a Christmas Miracle A Christmas story that will melt your heart
Pay-to-Go   America-First Immigration Fix
Legalizing Illegal Aliens Via Resident Visas Americans-first plan saves $Trillions. Learn how!
60 Million Illegal Aliens in America!!! A simple, America-first solution.
The Bill of Rights By Founder James Madison Refresh *your knowledge of the specific rights for all*
Great Players in Army Football Great Army Football played by great players..
Great Coaches in Army Football Army's coaches are all great.
Great Moments in Army Football Army Football at its best.
Great Moments in Florida Gators Football Gators Football from the start. This is the book.
Great Moments in Clemson Football CU Football at its best. This is the book.
Great Moments in Florida Gators Football Gators Football from the start. This is the book.
The Constitution Companion. A Guide to Reading and Comprehending the Constitution
The Constitution by Hamilton, Jefferson, & Madison – Big type and in English
PATERNO: The Dark Days After Win # 409. Sky began to fall within days of win # 409.
JoePa 409 Victories: Say No More! Winningest Division I-A football coach ever
American College Football: The Beginning From before day one football was played.
Great Coaches in Alabama Football Challenging the coaches of every other program!
Great Coaches in Penn State Football the Best Coaches in PSU's football program
Great Players in Penn State Football The best players in PSU's football program
Great Players in Notre Dame Football The best players in ND's football program
Great Coaches in Notre Dame Football The best coaches in any football program
Great Players in Alabama Football from Quarterbacks to offensive Linemen Greats!
Great Moments in Alabama Football AU Football from the start. This is the book.
Great Moments in Penn State Football PSU Football, start--games, coaches, players,
Great Moments in Notre Dame Football ND Football, start, games, coaches, players
Cross Country With the Parents A great trip from East Coast to West with the kids
Seniors, Social Security & the Minimum Wage. Things seniors need to know.
How to Write Your First Book and Publish It with CreateSpace
The US Immigration Fix--It's all in here. Finally, an answer.
I had a Dream IBM Could be #1 Again The title is self-explanatory
WineDiets.Com Presents The Wine Diet Learn how to lose weight while having fun.
Wilkes-Barre, PA; Return to Glory Wilkes-Barre City's return to glory
Geoffrey Parsons' Epoch... The Land of Fair Play Better than the original.
The Bill of Rights 4 Dummmies! This is the best book to learn about your rights.
Sol Bloom's Epoch ...Story of the Constitution The best book to learn the Constitution
America 4 Dummmies! All Americans should read to learn about this great country.
The Electoral College 4 Dummmies! How does it really work?
The All-Everything Machine Story about IBM's finest computer server.
ThankYou IBM! This book explains how IBM was beaten in the computer marketplace by neophytes

Brian has written 146 books in total. Other books can be found at amazon.com/author/brianwkelly

www.ingramcontent.com/pod-product-compliance
Lightning Source LLC
Chambersburg PA
CBHW070940280326
41934CB00009B/1952